How to Write a Covenant

BY BRENDA ZINTGRAFF

How to Write a Covenant
by Brenda Zintgraff

Printed in the United States of America.

ISBN 9781498452533

Scripture quotations taken from the American Standard Version (ASV)-*public domain*

Front Cover Photographer: Ginger McEowen

Back Cover Photographer: Kimberly Cheri Robinson

www.xulonpress.com

How to Write a Covenant

By Brenda Zintgraff

Edited by
Rachel Zintgraff

TABLE OF CONTENTS

DEDICATION

To Tom, the love of my life. I could have never accomplished this without your continuous encouragement and support. I love you.

I would also like to dedicate this book to our children: Christy, Ginger and James, as well as their children. They are the joy of my life and brought me into seeking the revelation of writing covenants. My children's children are my legacy and will carry this wisdom with them for generations to come.

ACKNOWLEDGEMENT

To my mother, Margie Rose Maltby

*O*ver the years, I discussed with her about my covenants and how God's word was so alive and active. She was amazed and sat with me many hours, talking about the new concept of writing covenants. I helped her to write covenants for her children and various situations in her life. Only a few months ago, before she was promoted to heaven, she placed a last request. She sat on the side of her bed and said to me, "Brenda, you have to finish the book. I will read it when I get to heaven."

After her passing into glory only a few months ago, I knew I had to finish the book and get it out there for others to glean from. I call my mother blessed.

ENDORSEMENTS

Many times, when I read a book, I wonder if this is an idea or if the writer has any real experience with the topic. I can say first hand, this book is Brenda's way of life. When she first started writing covenants to the Lord, she mentioned it to me and I saw them on the refrigerator. Little did I know, this was the beginning of a major change in me and my family. It was not just a change in lifestyle, but we saw the Father's hand in everything she wrote about. He did things we thought were completely impossible. Sometimes it was very humbling to realize I was making these vast improvements, only to find out she had written a covenant about that very thing months or even years earlier.

Now, if we are not writing or agreeing on the covenants, there seems to be something missing. It has become a lifestyle that we cannot live without. It is a part of our relationship with Him and it has brought us together. He is the center of all we do.

Brenda, thank you for being hungry enough to seek out revelation and faithfully walk this path with the Lord. It has blessed our family, and now others, beyond words.

I love YOU!

Tom Zintgraff

Husband, Pastor and Founder of Harvest Church

How to Write a Covenant was not written as a narrative about imaginary characters and events. Neither was it pinned by a novice, but rather is a recounting of a most valuable treasure fashioned in the heart that can only be the result of many years of living out what the author has conveyed in this book. This is her personal story of the tremendous power available when making covenants that are solely based upon the Word of Almighty God. The entire Bible is actually based upon the validity of our covenant making God. The Writer has seen the faithfulness of her God to keep covenant not only for herself but also to future generations. I Chronicles 16:15:'Be mindful of His covenant forever, the promise which He commanded and established to a thousand generations'. The Author has arranged a practical yet powerful unearthing as how to write a covenant that has the potential to bring the body of Christ into a new level of discovery of the power of covenant making. One not out of fear nor frustration of unanswered prayers, but firmly based upon the faithfulness of our Creator Who still today keeps covenant with those who will dare to believe His Eternal Word. I highly applaud our dear Mrs.

Zintgraff for allowing us to share such a treasure so precious as how to make a covenant with our Faithful God!

Samuel L. Brassfield
President and co-founder of Harvest International Ministries

There is nothing as powerful as praying God's Word. God watches over His Word to perform it (Jeremiah 1:12). His Word never returns void (Isaiah 55:12). If we ask anything ac-cording to His will (His Word reveals His will), He hears us and we will receive what we ask for (1 John 5:14,15).

I have been friends with Tom and Brenda Zintgraff for many years. I believe that this book she wrote holds one of the greatest keys to a successful prayer life. The book is timely for the hour in which we live. It is my prayer that everyone who reads it will be inspired to write down covenant prayers based on the Word of God. When you experience the power of this type of praying, you never will stop...and you will want to pass down how to do it to the next generation. I pray that God will raise up a nation of prayer warriors who will pray God's Word, birth revival, and turn our nation and families to God.

Rev. Woody Woodson
Woodson Ministries

FOREWORD

I chose the title of this book because I knew nothing about how to pray before the Holy Spirit revealed it to me through the writing of covenants, instead of whining, begging and complaining. I had no power in my prayers before this revelation was exposed to me. Only the Holy Spirit could have taught me such a revelation of the power of His word and how to put it into effect in my life.

Years ago, when I found myself really desperate and situations around me got so bad, I simply didn't know where to turn. I would go to my bedroom and throw myself onto the bed, bury my face in a pillow and cry out, "Oh, God! Fix it! God, fix it!"

Can you relate?

I simply didn't know how to pray effectively. My prayers were, as some have called it "bouncing off the ceiling."

Now I knew that God's word in Psalm 130:1-2 said, "When I cry unto You, Oh Lord, You hear my voice." But somehow I knew that I had a missing ingredient in my prayer life. It was thirty-six years ago, as a struggling wife and mother of two small children, that I found my answer to prayer in writing my first covenant. This was an event that changed my life forever. I have used the writing of covenants to teach my children and grand-children the power of His active word. Our destiny has been altered for eternity.

Hopefully, by writing this book, you can learn through my experience the power of His active word going forth and changing the atmosphere of your life.

Brenda Zintgraff

INTRODUCTION:

WHAT IS A COVENANT?

What is a covenant? ***Webster's Dictionary*** explains it as:

1. An agreement formally made
2. To pledge oneself, as to the performance of one's past in a pact
3. To agree or obligate by terms

*I*n today's world, a perfect example of a covenant is the title to a vehicle. You go to the loan officer and agree or obligate yourself to make payments over a period of time until the vehicle is completely paid in full. You even sign and date your name on a legal document, agreeing to make those payments faithfully. After shaking hands on your word of agreement, you begin to make endless payments until one day, after the last payment is made, you receive a title from the bank that says the vehicle is "PAID IN FULL." The vehicle becomes yours.

Taking a more serious step in covenant would be buying your first home. You go to a mortgage company and agree, in writing, to faithfully make payments for twenty to thirty years. You sign it and date it, and when you have finally made the last payment, you receive a "Guaranteed Title" on your home with your very own name on that title and a date that seals it as yours.

Marriage is another type of covenant. When you choose your spouse, you step into a new covenant of marriage through the vows you speak publicly. You even sign a legal marriage certificate, but that vow is made with the heart. Our society has many such written covenants that we make choices to enter.

The greatest covenant is the written covenant of God's word.

Before receiving this revelation of writing covenants, I had never actually written my own name on God's word and come into agreement with it. But, thirty-six years ago, I did just that. I wrote my first covenant and watched God hasten to perform His word on my behalf. I began to write, sign and date the written word of the Lord. When I saw the speed with which God's word came to pass, my life took a complete change.

Chapter One

HIS WORD IS ALIVE!

Thirty-six years ago, I discovered a new scripture: Hebrews 4:12. The revelation of this one verse in God's word became alive to me and changed my life forever.

Hebrews 4:12 says, "The word of God is *alive* and *active*. Sharper than a double-edged sword; It penetrates even to the dividing of soul and spirit; the joints and marrow; it judges the thoughts and attitudes of the heart."

Now, as a young wife and mother of two children, my fears and thoughts were always wrapped around my immediate situations: my husband, his job, my kids, money, bills, health, my home, etc. My prayers were extensive complaints. I found myself explaining to God on a daily basis how unfair things were. I would say, "Oh, God, Tom (my husband) needs a raise! It's just not fair that Joe got a raise and a promotion and my husband works a lot harder than him. We need more money, too, God! I can't pay the bills! Fix it! Do you hear me, God? Fix it!"

I would plead with and whine to God and explain to Him all the situations I was in, just in case He couldn't see them. I longed to fix up my house, yet there was never enough money. I would tell the Lord all these things.

I had two beautiful little girls, ages one and two. I didn't want my kids to be like me. I wanted better for them. You see, I had a lot of fear and rejection in my life. I didn't want my children to struggle in school with grades and peer pressure, like I had, so I would complain to the Lord in the same way, "Oh God, make my kids smart!"

I didn't want my children to have the same struggles and insecurities that I had, but I didn't know how to pray for them and get results. I found my prayers were worries and fears about what might happen. They had no power. I call them "Brenda Prayers."

I wanted more for my children than I had for myself. Most moms want the same, yet, this is how most moms pray for their children. They lift up their worries to the Lord and walk away from their prayer time feeling discouraged or wondering if God ever really heard that prayer.

I had read in the Psalms that He heard my cry and He would answer me. I believe He did hear my cry and, by His Holy Spirit, gave me a revelation.

I praise God that this revelation came at just the right time in my life. When I read in Hebrews 4:12 that God's word was alive and active, it just simply shocked me. I thought, "Oh my gosh!" It had never occurred to me that His word was actually alive. And it is active! This whole thought process was just rolling over and over in my mind. *His word is alive! His word is active!*

You see, I knew that God's word was true. And I knew that His word was for us today. I even understood that I had to believe it. However, I saw God's word as a history book full of neat old stories. Somehow I missed the whole reality that His word was alive and active. I missed the fact that His word went forth and penetrated. This was what had to be seen as I began to put it into action.

My dad had knelt with me years ago at the altar of the church and showed me the scriptures in Romans 10:9-10, that if I confessed with my mouth that Jesus is Lord, and believed in my heart that God raised Jesus from the dead, then I would be saved. I had confessed Jesus Christ as Lord of my life and believed that God had raised Him from the dead. That happened years ago. But, I simply got a revelation this particular day that His word was alive and active. This new revelation was rolling on the inside of me with a hunger and an accelerating speed. This whole revelation created a new desire to put His word on paper and agree with it. If the word of God really was alive and it really did penetrate to the soul and spirit, and even to the joints and marrow of the bones, then something very serious was about to change my life. If His word really was alive, my envisioned future was about to change. I was about to write, sign and seal it with a date. I thought, *I will write a contract with God.* A COVENANT was revealed.

Important!

CHAPTER TWO

MY FIRST COVENANT

$\mathcal{I}$ was a twenty-seven-year-old mother at home with a one-year-old and a two-year-old daughter. Both girls were unique in their very own way. The oldest daughter, Christy, had bright red hair. From the day she was born, everyone told me that she would be hot-tempered. I was warned continually that I would really have to keep a watch out for her because of her red hair. "That red-head is going to be hot-tempered! Everyone will make fun of her. Poor little Christy."

At that time, I could feel the fear entering my mind of not knowing what to do or how to handle such a horrible curse. As my precious red-head began to grow, I watched her play with her younger sister, Ginger. She would try to hug her and it seemed that every time she just tried to love on her, Christy would stumble and accidently knock my one-year-old over. Soon, little Ginger had bumps and bruises from Christy accidentally being too rough. I began to hear everyone around me telling me how Christy was just going through an awkward age. I began to see clumsiness in her. I again feared the hot temper and the ridicule my little girl would get from others. My love for my children was extraordinary and I wanted only the best for them.

Since Hebrews 4:12 said that His word was alive and active, I decided to go to my Bible and find scriptures in my concordance that were the opposite of these awful remarks being spoken over my daughter. I looked up gentleness. Sure enough, under the word "gentle," I found many scriptures. So, I chose two scriptures and I wrote them down on a 3" x 5" index card with Christy's name on it. It read:

November 1980

Christy

2 Timothy 2:24 The servant of the Lord must not strive but be gentle unto all men, apt to teach and patient…
Psalm 18:35 Thy gentleness hath made Christy great!

Shortly thereafter, I began to see change taking place in my two-year-old. I watched as gentleness began to manifest its beauty in Christy. My little red-head was becoming a tender and gentle person. As the word of God was written over her, we watched as God created His gentleness of perfection. God dropped a love for ballet into Christy at an early age. Gracefulness rose in her spirit as she found a new love for dance and trained with a ballet company in her younger years. People began to call her graceful and gentle.

I didn't even realize how much was in that little scripture of 2 Timothy 2:24. I simply wanted her to be gentler. The gentleness came and hot tempers were not a part of our family lifestyle. But as time went on, I realized that Christy had a new gift of teaching and counsel as she talked to her friends and helped them. When I went back and read the small covenant, I realized part of that verse said "apt to teach" as well as "patient." Since that time, I have realized through revelation exactly what God was doing in my red-head.

Thirty-six years have passed and I have seen that gift of teaching pour out of her as she counsels and teaches young women today all over the United States. Christy and her husband, Eric, have been young married directors in our church and she is now director over women's activities. I had the privilege to sit and listen to her Bible study on "How to make a House a Home" last week. I have watched this little clumsy red-head develop into a beautiful, graceful and gentle woman who teaches God's word and counsels at a mighty level, all because of the word of God that went forth and penetrated her heart and the marrow of her bones at age two.

Christy knew at an early age, even before marriage, that she would have four children. She had a heart to be a mother and wife and raise four children of her own. Christy began writing covenants at an early age and had to believe God at His word, as I did. She was very patient as she put her husband through college as well as medical school. After ten years, they had their first child. Talk about patience being perfected! Many covenants were written during those years. Today, she has four beautiful children and a loving and faithful husband. Another generation is rising up to watch God perform His written word.

Now, on the back side of that same index card that I wrote for Christy, I wrote a different choice of scriptures for my younger daughter. You see, Ginger was only one-and-a-half years old, and I was beginning to see a lot of my own insecurities in her. Every time anyone would come up to Ginger and speak to her, she would hide behind my skirts and bury her face in her hands in shame. The shyness was so severe that Ginger wouldn't even look at people when they spoke to her. People began to say," Oh, she's so shy!" I also saw that Ginger simply would not talk. She would make hand signals for what she wanted, and Christy would interpret her unidentified words and hand signals for us. I feared that my one-and-a-half-year-old would never speak fluently.

I knew that Jesus was NOT a shy person. He was bold as a lion, and when He went about speaking God's word to all who would listen, it was powerful! So shyness was not a good quality in my book. I went to the concordance in the back of my Bible and began to look up scriptures on boldness and confidence, since these words were the opposite of shy. I flipped the same 3" x 5" index card over and wrote this:

November 1980

Ginger

> 2 Timothy 1:7 - For God hath not given Ginger the spirit of fear; but of power and love and of a sound mind.
> Philippians 1:14 - Make her more bold to speak the word of God without fear.

The next thing I did was take the little index card and put it on my refrigerator with a magnet, so I could see it each day and agree with it. I had just written my first covenant.

Little did I know that the words on that index card were going to go forth and penetrate the joints and marrow of my little girls' bones and change their lives forever. It was only two weeks later from the day I wrote my first covenant that the change became very evident in my youngest child.

My husband and I had begun hosting home group Bible studies each week during this season. Scripture songs were very popular in the Christian world of the 70s, and it was a new era of the move of the Holy Spirit. One afternoon, a lady named Shirley Emmons came to my door for our Friday night home group and Bible study. My one-year-old was standing behind me when she came into the living room. To my surprise, Ginger stepped out from behind my skirt and said, "Ya wanna hear me sing a song?" Of course, the woman said yes, and Ginger began to sing in a faint childlike voice, "The word of faith is nigh thee even in my mouth."

This was a scripture song that we sang in our home group. Ginger had heard these songs over and over. I know that my mouth dropped open as I watched the boldness come forth from my one-and-a-half-year-old daughter. I literally watched as the word of God was sung boldly from her lips. God is so faithful! His word had gone forth and penetrated the heart and marrow of Ginger's bones. I had done absolutely nothing to make that happen. God's word did it all. Two weeks had passed since I wrote this covenant on my little index card. Only two weeks! My little girl was already speaking, as well as singing, the word of God!

Years later, this shy little girl became bolder and bolder. As God began to develop her and pour new gifts and talents into her, she became a national gymnast, a cheerleader, and a singer who sang in state choir. She had a gift of music and picked up the bass guitar and also played drums. She marched in the band and went to state as well. Her senior year of high school, she was nominated Homecoming Queen. What an honor for the small, insecure one-year-old of the past. So much more happened because of that one covenant that words cannot tell. Tom and I watched God's word coming forth boldly without fear, just as the covenant had said. Years later, His word was still being performed in her.

Now, that little girl is married and raising two beautiful daughters in the Lord. Ginger and her godly and faithful husband have implemented covenants into their family's lives as well. She is watching daily as God performs His word in their children (my grandchildren).

Covenants have also become a part of Ginger's children as they write covenants for life-changing events. At grade school age, they care about their friends and teachers. They understand the power and activity of

God's word. It is a way of life for our family for three generations now.

God is still, to this very day, hastening to perform His word, even in my grandchildren. His word is still alive and active. That never changes. What would my children be like today if I had not written that simple covenant on a 3" x 5" index card years ago? Would I even have grandchildren today, who walk with God and have His great favor on their lives?

What was so beautiful about writing God's word on the index card was that my little girls did not KNOW that I had written a covenant for them. They were not standing there, saying, "Oh dear, Mom's praying for us again. We really need to change our ways and become more bold and gentle." No! They were only one and two years old. They were just living their own little lives while God's word was actively going forth and penetrating their souls and spirits. His word was alive then as it is now! It never stopped being alive! It never stopped being active!

I found myself just wrapping myself in God's word.

"Wow," I would say to myself, "I am changing our destiny! I am changing it through the word of God." Continuous revelation was coming forth about how alive and active His word really is.

His word became more and more a part of my life. I could see God doing things, and everything became so much more real to me. There were so many times I had needs and I loved trusting the word and writing covenants. I began a folder of all the covenants I had written and I dated and signed every one.

One day, I saw that the girls needed some new clothes. They had outgrown everything and money was still scarce at this point in my life. I had just recently discovered the scripture, "Give and it shall be given unto you, pressed down, shaken together and running over" (Luke 6:38). I quickly wrote the covenant of need and told the girls, "We need to give away your clothes that are too small and God will supply our need for new ones. He will give back to us, pressed down and running over." This was a learning time for my children early on.

They were only about three and four at this time, but they were willing and eager to give. I took the scripture and placed it on the old clothes and prayed for a return from God. I wanted the girls could see what God would do. We gave the clothes away, and three days later, a neighbor who lived across from my in-laws called. She asked if I wanted some clothes for my girls. I was excited and couldn't wait to see what she would bring! When they brought seven huge boxes of beautiful clothes, the girls and I were overjoyed. There were enough clothes in perfect condition for five years of growth for my two girls. There were beautiful dresses and play clothes in perfect condition. This was such a happy day as we tried on new clothes for hours. This was such a faith builder for my children. God was faithful once again. "Pressed down, shaken together and running over" was experienced over and over in our lives.

CHAPTER THREE

PROMOTION FOR TOM

*A*fter seeing God's word come to pass so quickly for my children, I thought, *Wow, there are some things in my husband, Tom, that really need to be fixed.* I had prayed over the years in a very similar way as I had for my girls. There was no scripture or power behind my prayers for Tom. I simply worried and feared for my husband, as so many women do.

Tom was a hard worker. He had landed a job in Houston with the railroad and was at the bottom of the totem pole. He loved God with all his heart. He had not yet been called into the ministry, but we went to church regularly and he worked very hard at whatever he did in the workforce. I remember going to the Lord because we needed money, and saying, "Lord, give Tom a promotion!" or "Lord, give Tom a raise." I was very frustrated and I prayed with a begging mentality. I literally worried on my knees!

When his coworker—let's call him Joe—would get the promotion instead of Tom, I would go back to the Lord and cry out, "Lord! Joe doesn't deserve that promotion! *My* husband works so much harder than Joe! Tom deserved to be promoted! *Not Joe.*"

I complained and explained to God what He had already heard a hundred times before, but nothing changed. So, I decided to write a covenant for Tom. I wanted to see results in my prayers for my husband, as any woman would want.

Things had changed so drastically with my girls that I had set in my heart to write a covenant that lined up with God's word for Tom. I went to the word of God for my new covenant called *Tom*. I did the exact same thing that I had done with Christy and Ginger and wrote on a 3" x 5" index card. It read:

TOM

Psalm 1:3

Tom is like a tree planted by the water, yielding his fruit in due season. His leaves do not wither. Whatever Tom sets his hands to shall prosper.

2 Corinthians 8:7-8
Cause Tom to abound in everything... In faith, utterance, in knowledge and in love.

Luke 2:52
Jesus increased in wisdom and stature and in favor with God and man.

Joshua 1:8
Cause Tom to meditate in God's word day and night and to observe it and make all his ways prosperous. Cause him to find favor in the eyes of those in authority over him.
(This was a key scripture that changed the scales the quickest)

Now this was as simple as it gets. But, as before, I had no idea how much revelation and knowledge were in these three little scriptures. A whole new world was set in motion because of the ALIVE and ACTIVE word that was going forth.

The favor of God was not residing on Tom's life before this covenant was written. Tom had done well at every job he ever had. He had worked in a grocery store as a young boy and a children's television station in high school. He was drafted into the United States

Navy at age eighteen and succeeded by his own efforts. He worked hard and was very respectful to his boss and those in authority over him, but that anointed favor of God Almighty was now being spoken over Tom and declared into the atmosphere. His word was now alive and active and was going forth. A supernatural change was taking place as I took my little 3"x 5" card with my new declaration and agreed with it. I agreed with God's alive and active word for the favor of God to reside upon my husband.

I was impatient. I wanted God to "hurry up" and perform His word.

"Hurry up, God!" I would cry out. And we all know that when we cry unto the Lord, He will answer. And He did! Again, I simply didn't have the right words to pray, but in my desperation, the Holy Spirit miraculously took me to the scripture. Jeremiah 1:12:

I will hasten my word to perform it!

Wow, what a revelation I got right then and there! God did not hasten to perform "Brenda's words." He hastened to perform HIS word. And He would perform it in Tom Zintgraff. Oh my goodness, this was incredible! There is nothing in the world like receiving revelation knowledge from the Holy Spirit and understanding the word in a supernatural way. It is absolutely addicting!

Within only a short time, change began to take place. The favor of God began to become evident to both Tom and me. Tom was coming home and telling me about his day at work and how God helped him to solve problems like never before. His boss was asking him to take on more and more responsibility, and the favor was increasing daily. Tom began to look forward to going to work to see what the Lord had for his day. Promotion came and financial blessing took place. We began to see a supernatural authority become evident in Tom. There was actually an authority that rode upon his shoulders, and people saw it.

I no longer had to beg God for the next promotion. Tom was recognized quickly by those in authority over him, and found himself next in line for promotion without question. Compliments began to flood his evaluations. This had been accomplished though God's word. His word was alive and active and had gone forth, once again, and accomplished that which pleased the Lord! Tom found promotion and gaining favor was easier than ever before. I was excited to see my husband come home and share all the news of the day. God was faithful once again.

CHAPTER FOUR

THE NEW JOURNEY

As I watched the hand of God move in Tom's life, the day came that God called him into the ministry. I will never forget that day as long as I live. We were attending a huge mega church in Houston, Texas called Evangelistic Temple. It was a normal Sunday as we got ready for services. Our pastor and the board had decided to start a school of ministry for those who had a call on their lives. I remember him getting up on the platform and telling about all the plans of what this program involved.

These were the days of revival and the Spirit of God moved suddenly and at the most unusual times. This was one of those times. Everyone got quiet and we just knew that something great was about to happen. The pastor said, "Someone here today is being called of God, right now!" There were about 3,000 people sitting out there in the audience, including Tom and me. We were all looking around to see who this person was. Then, the pastor said," Where are you? Who is the man that God is calling out? Get down here right now so I can pray for you!"

Tom and I were still looking around to see who this blessed person might be. And then, it happened. The Holy Spirit showed up when we least expected it. Tom began to shake all over, from the top of his head all the way to his toes. I looked at him and wondered if he was having a convulsion or something. I grabbed his hand to try to settle him down. His eyes were closed and he just kept shaking like a rabid Chihuahua!

Then the pastor said, "There he is! Right there! Get yourself down here, son!" He was pointing right at my husband. I was mortified! Tom just shook all the harder until he slid off the pew and onto the floor. He could not stand up and he began to crawl to the front of the church. I held my hand over the side of my face and tried to act as though I had no idea who in the world this person was. Yet, somehow, I remembered the covenant that I had written. I wondered if there was a scripture in there somewhere with revelation I had not yet discovered that said something about the ministry. He was the only person who went up for the call that morning. The pastor and elders of the church prayed over Tom and this set in motion the act of faith to follow the call of God.

Tom started attending the school of ministry internship. Later, at least ten other men rose up to become a part of this new intern program at Evangelistic Temple as well.

This was a major event that changed the course of our lives. Tom began to devour the word of God. Revelation came full force while meditating in God's word. Tom was becoming like a tree firmly planted by the water, bringing forth fruit in due season. He was abounding. I saw the favor increase in all that he set his hands to. It had to be the word going forth, even more powerful than I ever dreamed. The covenant was coming forth, alive and active, in my husband. His word was not returning void!

When the school came to an end, God was ready to move us on to new things. We wondered when He would drop a huge mega church in our lap and we would start our ministry. What we didn't know was that we had to be prepared and seasoned. We didn't understand that being in the ministry didn't necessarily mean we had to have a church. We had so much to learn about God, the Holy Spirit, and obedience. Our journey had just begun.

CHAPTER FIVE

A COVENANT FOR BRENDA

I watched the favor ride on Tom's shoulders with many opportunities. God's word was being performed in him over and over. I saw all these things happening in my children, my husband, and our circumstances. I prayed in a new way that was changing our finances, our future, and our destiny.

I was writing journals of covenants and watching God's word come forth at an accelerated rate. I was dating each and every covenant and signing them as if they were valuable contracts between me and God. I was desiring more and more of the promises of God and developing a relationship with my heavenly Father that was priceless. I wanted to impart this new knowledge to my children and hang on to it for eternity. However, I knew that I needed to see some changes in my own life. It was time for me to look at the ugly things in myself that I had not conquered and write a covenant for my life. *How scary!* We all know that it is much easier to believe that a prayer can be heard and answered for someone else, but when it comes to our own lives, we accept the hidden, ugly things. We feel as if we cannot change ourselves and be healed and conquered. When it comes to us, it's a different story.

God had been so faithful through the covenants I wrote over Christy, Ginger and my husband, Tom, but I questioned if God wanted His word performed in me. Of course He did! So, it was time. I had to write a covenant over Brenda.

Growing up, I had very low self-esteem. I was extremely shy around people, especially popular kids, whom I thought were throwing up an air of conceit and arrogance. Like every other teenager, I yearned to be accepted. I simply didn't know the right things to say that would make people like me. So, I preferred to stay away from crowds, which made me come across as snobbish and stuck up. I was not smart in school, and being smart was a big deal, as far as I was concerned. If you wanted to be anyone, you had to be smart. If you wanted to do sports, which I loved, if you wanted to be nominated for an office in student council or be a cheerleader, you had to be smart. If you wanted to do anything in school, you had to make the grade.

It seemed hopeless for me to ever be a part of any extra-curricular activities because of my lack in the grades. I struggled tremendously in this area. I could not grasp how to study or take tests. Reading was my poorest subject. I can honestly tell you I had only read five books in my life from cover to cover when I graduated from high school. Book reports freaked me out. I would always find someone who had read the book and have them tell me all about it, so I could then write a report that barely pulled off the passing grade. As far as oral book reports went, I was mortified to stand in front of a class and talk. So, I literally got sick on the day of oral reports. I remember a kind English teacher allowing me to come in after school one day to do my oral report for her, because she recognized my fear of standing in front of my peers. I didn't have the knowledge of how to put God's word into effect in my life and make things change on my own behalf. After all, I was just a teenager in the 60s, trying to fit in.

I cheated on tests and wept when the report cards came out every six weeks. Even graduating from high school created a fear that consumed me. I took summer school classes every summer to slide by for another year. I always wondered if people knew that I was the dumb kid who didn't pass the test. My insecurity was pathetic, and I remember walking with my head hanging low and shielding myself with my books as I went from class to class. I suppose this was my way of hiding from the outside world.

The devil has a way of putting thoughts in your head that are lies. I didn't even know there was a devil, and I certainly didn't know I was influenced by him. Though I dreaded to bring that report card home every six weeks, I did graduate from H.M. King High School. I always thought maybe they just passed me because I never caused a problem or made trouble.

To this day, I am very proud of my diploma. Back then, if I had the knowledge of God's word and could have applied it, oh, the things I could have accomplished! Because of this secret past, I decided to go to the Lord and confess, as well as write, a covenant about my greatest desire: to be SMART. From the depths of my soul, I asked, "Lord, what is smart in Your word? How do I become smart?"

At that very moment, the Holy Spirit just dropped the answer into my spirit. Deep down, I knew that I knew I had the answer. Wisdom! Wisdom! Wisdom! It rang in my spirit so loud and clear. I went to the book of wisdom in the Bible called Proverbs. I was very honest with God and told Him that I didn't like to read. However, I poured myself into the book of Proverbs and began to study this wise book.

Now, most women have at least heard of Proverbs, and most Christian women have read Proverbs, but did they read it over and over and write it down and make covenants with it? Did they date it and sign it? Did they agree with it? I dare say that most women probably couldn't say, "Yes! This book is for *me*!" Had anyone actually taken this wisdom book and applied it in writing? Had they watched God's word go forth and pierce their heart with the truth? As a matter of fact, I have found that most women believe the Proverbs woman is an unrealistic fantasy.

I became obsessed with the book of Proverbs. I knew that the Holy Spirit had given me a new love to read and absorb the words on the pages. I felt regenerated from the revelation that poured out of the book. I knew that I was actually learning to read as I read. My mind was being renewed from God's word. For the first time in my life, I didn't care about being smart any more. I just wanted all that God could give to me in this one book. I made up my mind right then and there: I was going to be a Proverbs woman. I wrote down every single thing I wanted when I saw it. Proverbs 31 was by far my favorite chapter. I felt compelled to apply it and allow God to make it happen in me. This was the answer I had needed all those years. Satan had made me feel so dumb in school, and put so much insecurity in me, that failure was inevitable. Now, I knew I could be so much more through God and His alive and active word. So, I wrote my first covenant for Brenda.

January 1981

BRENDA

Proverbs 31

My dear Lord and Savior:

I desire with all my heart to be wise. I desire Your wisdom book to become a part of my being.

Forgive me for only wanting the "smarts" of this world. Forgive me for waiting so long to turn to You. I give my rejection and all my insecurity to You. My fears, take them from me. Replace all the ugly parts of my being with Your word.

I desire to be a Proverbs woman. Create in me this woman of God who is of noble character. A woman of God whom my husband has full confidence in. Show me how to speak with wisdom and teach me how to have faithful instruction on my tongue. I desire to have no fear of tomorrow. Create in me all these things that please You. Thank You, Lord.

I trust You to do in me what You have done in my girls and in my husband.

I desire that one day, my children will rise up and call me blessed.

I need You, Lord. I need Your word to
become alive and active in my bones.
Amen

I wrote another covenant, and then another, as I
watched God's word come to pass on my behalf. There
were so many covenants that came to pass. His alive
and active word drove out so much rejection and shame.
But, I want to share a particular covenant I wrote in
1996. You see, even fifteen years later, I was still writing
covenants about becoming a Proverbs woman. God
was, and still is, perfecting His work in me. This is one
of my favorites that was life-changing and helped me to
move on without fear of failure as I watched His word
come to pass by agreement with His word. I had to continue to stand.

BRENDA 1996

I desire to be a Proverbs woman. The
kind of woman I read about in Your word,
oh Lord. I choose not to worry over my
children, but to trust You. Make me to be
clothed with strength and dignity. I can
laugh at the days to come. Cause me
to speak with wisdom and cause faithful
instruction to be on my tongue. Show me

how to watch over the affairs of my household and not to eat the bread of idleness.
I desire that my children rise up and they
will call me blessed. And my husband, he
will praise me. May I surpass all noble
women. Let me not charm them, but let
me be a woman who fears God. That is
why I will be praised. Give me the reward
that I have earned and let my works bring
me praise at the city gates. May my husband find full confidence in me...

Amen

All of these things were in full agreement with
Proverbs 31. The covenant goes on and on, lining up
with the word of the Lord. I dated it and signed it, just
like a contract. I agreed with God's word, which is alive
and active and going forth. I never came out of the contract. I never disagreed with the word of the Lord. His
word is His word. It is final authority.

God's word was continuing to grow inside of me. I
began to change and really believe His word was alive
in me. The Holy Spirit began to reveal to me that *smart*
was not what I needed at all. I had obtained a little bit
of wisdom from His word that was far more valuable. I
began to realize that just being smart was "head knowledge." I give God the glory for this valuable revelation

that the Holy Spirit brings through seeking Him and craving His word. Only the word of the Lord could be so active and alive that it could be performed in someone as simple as me.

CHAPTER SIX

OUR MARRIAGE

*A*fter watching God's word come to pass over and over, I wanted perfection in our marriage. Shortly after I had seen evidence of His word coming to pass in my family, I decided to write covenants over our marriage. I want you to see one of the first covenants I wrote over Tom and me. I must say, once again, we had immediate results.

1981

OUR MARRIAGE

Lord, Help Tom and me to have a new love, that no one can separate us from the love of Christ. I will say with my mouth, WE shall walk in love and we shall have the fruits of the Spirit: love, peace, joy,

gentleness, goodness, faith, meekness,
and we shall live in the Spirit of the Lord.
Amen

I have written dozens of new covenants as we come upon new events in our lives. God continues to honor His word each and every time.

Tom and I counsel many couples today who know absolutely nothing about writing covenants, and we hear them say the same things over and over. "Oh my gosh, if my wife was only this…" or, "If my husband was only that…" or "Just help us fix our marriage." These are the same words and complaining that I had once done.

This first covenant was one of many that changed our marriage. I have to make a bold statement here: If you do not really want these things for your life, your wife, your husband or your children, then do not pray the word of God over them. I cannot say this enough: God's word is *alive* and *active* and it will go forth and it will be accomplished.

CHAPTER SEVEN

THE PROCESS

"*C*ause Tom to abound in everything."

This was something I saw so clearly. He was abounding in everything.

He was called into the ministry about the time my girls were two and three years of age, just shortly after I began to write covenants over him. It was always in the back of his mind, "I can't wait to have a church and be in my ministry." But Tom was working for many companies before we ever stepped over into being pastors of a church. It was years!

It was a process before we actually had a church. Tom talks about the process all the time. We went through a training time before he actually became a pastor. The process took twenty years. We had to be trained and raised up for the perfect season that God had for us.

During this season of being prepared for the ultimate plan and purpose of God, I continued to write covenants over my children. When Christy and Ginger were about nine and ten years old, I decided to write a covenant for their husbands. I had heard so many horror stories about in-laws. I loved my kids so much and I wanted them to be a part of my life forever. I didn't want them to just get married and move off and never see them again. I desired that their husbands would be awesome for my daughters and they would love Tom and me.

So in 1989, I wrote a covenant for Christy and Ginger's future husbands. In 1989, Christy was twelve years old.

Christy Zintgraff's Husband

Cause Christy to dwell in the secret place of the Most High and to abide under the shadow of the almighty. Cover her with Your feathers. She will not be afraid, for she will know the will of God. He will be her shield and cause her to sing praises unto the Lord all the days of her life... And choose Christy's husband and mold him and make him especially for her. For he will love her as Christ loved the church and give Himself for it. He will cleave to her and sanctify her. Cause him to cherish her and make him holy. Give Christy and this man that You have chosen for her a long and happy life together.

Amen

Now as time went on, Christy and Ginger both began to write covenants as well. They could see the value and success of trusting God's word and writing down important issues in their lives. They desired things to come to pass for various situations as they came up. They wrote covenants for their teachers, their friends, and many other circumstances.

They wanted to see friends come to know Jesus as well. They wanted to find favor with their teachers. They wrote about grades and decisions that were important. They wrote covenants because they saw Tom and me do this, and the results were incredible. But what I had implemented in their lives was the ability to do it themselves! This is so important for the heritage to be passed on.

Tom and I have trained our children and the people of our church to be warriors in the spirit realm. We truly believe that as Christians we should know how to fight in the battles that come before us. If we have not been trained, then we will be overcome in the fight. His word is our weapon.

I will never forget one Monday morning. Ginger, my youngest daughter came to our home very early for coffee. She said, "Dad, you said something on Sunday morning in your sermon that struck me. You were talking about David in the Bible and you said, 'Giant killers train giant killers.' I thought, hmm... my dad is a GREAT giant killer. He knows about fighting spiritual battles. This word is for strong people, not someone like me. But your words have stayed with me throughout the night and when I woke this morning, I thought, 'Why *not* me?' I decided to ask the Lord if I could be a giant killer too. I *want* to be a giant killer. So, I asked God to make me a giant killer like David. Thank you, Dad, for having the faith in me, even before I did."

God was certainly in this little unplanned coffee time. A major impartation took place that morning in May. Ginger, this giant killer in training, prayed for her dad that day. By faith, she stood up boldly and took a warrior stance behind her dad as though she had a sword in her hand. As I watched, I saw this warrior taking authority over the enemy. She prayed for strength as an amour bearer. The power of God was upon us and there was no doubt Ginger had crossed over to a new spiritual level. Tom then imparted to Ginger the anointing to be the amour bearer. It was a glorious "May Day" at war. A battle was won.

Our children watch and learn. As you write covenants for your children, you never know what the Holy Spirit will do tomorrow in their hearts. A request was granted once again.

CHAPTER EIGHT

COVENANTS FOR SPOUSES

One day, my oldest daughter, Christy decided to write a covenant for her future husband. I believe she was about fifteen years old. She was very detailed about her desires and the fact that he had to line up with the word of God. She almost drove me crazy because she added to her covenant daily. When she saw godly qualities she admired in a young man, she put them in her writings.. Here is a small interpretation of her covenant in my own words.

Christy's Future Husband

Lord, I want my husband to be smart! I don't want a dumb husband! I want him to be tall and I want him to have dark hair.

I want him to have a heart after God. I desire him to be fit and to be an athlete. I want him to run and not be weary and for him to have a love for sports. But I also want him to write poetry for me as Solomon did. I want him to love to dine at dinner theaters, and take me to operas and ballets also.

Now I was thinking, "Good Lord! Where do you find an athlete who writes poetry?!" But she did find her husband and he has a heart after God and he is an athlete. And would you believe, he writes poetry for her!

Christy and her husband, Eric

Now in 1989, the same time I wrote a covenant for Christy, I also wrote a covenant for Ginger's husband. She was only ten years old at that time. I wrote:

Ginger's Future Husband

Father, in Jesus' name, cause Ginger's voice to magnify You. Give her so many talents. Lift her hands to glorify You. Thank You for teaching her how to put the full armor of God upon herself. And I praise You for recreating a new Ginger with boldness of You inside.

(Ha! I am still agreeing with my original covenant for Ginger to be bold ten years later).

Holy Spirit, cause Ginger to seek after You and give her the baptism of the Holy Spirit and cause her to receive it gladly. And choose her husband right now, wherever he is and prepare him for marriage to my daughter.
Create in him even now to desire to be in complete harmony with You and Your word. Choose a husband that will love her as Christ loved the church and gave

Himself for it. Keep him pure and may this man be raised in a Christian home that loves God.

This was a simple declaration for my ten-year-old daughter that came to pass twelve years later to the exact letter.

Now, Ginger was very shy and insecure in the past, but from the covenants, declarations and standing, she attained that boldness that I had agreed upon. God's word went forth into her heart and began to change her over the years more and more. She became a new creature in Christ.

When Ginger was about eighteen years old, she decided to write a covenant for her future husband, since Christy had been quite successful with obtaining her heart's desire.

This scared the tar out of me! You see, she was our FUN child and I knew she wanted someone FUN! Ginger's covenant went something like this:

My future husband

I want a husband that is very tall and strong; someone who will protect me. I want a protector. And I want him to have favor and authority on him as my dad does. He must be a man of God and be pure and have excellent morals. He must love to have FUN! He must have the same interests that I have. He must be faithful and love me as Christ loved the church and gave Himself for it.

This was a simple covenant and to the point. But our God is faithful and saw the desire of her heart. Ginger's husband, Tyler, is a police officer and very loyal. He was also a national gymnast and helps coach and judge competitions with Ginger. He is the protector she desired and, most of all, has a heart after God. He has high moral standards and is competitive but loves to have FUN.

God is so faithful! He cares about our heart's desires and God puts desires in our hearts that line up with His word. He only wants the very best for us.

Ginger and her husband, Tyler

JAMES
1987

When I was about thirty-six years old, my girls were nine and ten years old, and I was pregnant with our son, James. Tom and I knew we were going to have a son and we were planning to name him James Thomas. We had believed God for our son to come into this world for ten years. Since covenants had become so much of a lifestyle, I wanted to write one for my son who was soon to come into this world.

I began to write…

Lord, I want my son to have a heart like David. Put in his heart to speak Your word boldly without fear from a young age. I want him to have a heart after You, Oh Lord. I desire my son to be strong, and bold as a lion. I desire him to be a speaker of truth. And even if he is small in stature, give him a supernatural strength, as You did David. Make him 'quick' as David was quick to take out the lion and the bear when they came after the sheep. Give him supernatural gifts. Place Your supernatural favor upon him at a very young age. I desire him to be so much like David that he even LOOKS like David. May he have a ruddy complexion as David had.

James came into our lives and he had red hair and the ruddy complexion. He was only four years old when he asked Jesus into his heart. He and his dad sat at the dining room table in front of a huge glass window as they talked about the importance of asking Jesus into your heart. I remember James telling this small testimony. He had hoped Jesus was really living inside of his heart, so he asked God that day if it was really true, and Jesus was really living inside of his heart, to let a star fall from the sky so he could know for sure. It was still daylight outside and about 5:30 in the evening. But a star fell across the sky that day, at that very moment, just for him to know that God had heard his prayer. James was so shocked, he asked God to "do it again!" And God did. A second star fell across the sky right then and there. It was a miracle. James wept that day for his friends who might not know Jesus. He was telling his friends in the neighborhood and at school about Jesus at an early age. God put a burden for the lost in James at the young age of four.

The favor of God was on James just as the covenant was written. God had given him supernatural gifts. He was quick and agile. He had a natural gift for golf at a very young age. He loved baseball, basketball, hockey and football. When he reached his high school years, he fell in love with a sport called paintball. But although the sports were evident in his life, everyone recognized a God-given favor that rode on James. His love for truth grew and the favor increased. There was boldness in him and he was not afraid to stand up in front of people and speak.

Recognizing the effectiveness of writing covenants, James also began to write to the Lord.

At a young age he believed he was James Bond. We laughed about that, but he also wanted a BMW Z3 like James Bond. This was impossible for Tom and me to just go out and buy a vehicle for James. God was going to have to handle this gift. James didn't tell too many people, to avoid conflict. He began to save for it at the age of fourteen, and by the time he was seventeen years old, he bought his dream car. Yes, he bought a BMW Z3. We gave God the glory for these little blessings that came along. God supernaturally stepped into the picture and made a way for James to have this request. Now you must understand that writing covenants is not a wish list for material things. But God did get the glory for this far out desire. Psalm 1:3 says to meditate in His word day and night and be like a tree firmly planted by the water, bringing forth fruit in due season. He will meet the desires of your heart. I believe James' heart was right as he was reading God's word and sharing the gospel with his friends. God simply saw the desire and knew He would get the glory. A very neat testimony of God's goodness.

When my son was about four years old, I wanted to write a covenant for his wife as I had for my daughters. I wanted his wife to like me and Tom, and for us to get along well, and I wanted her to be greatly loved by James' sisters.

So I wrote a covenant for James' wife, Rachel, who was not even born yet at the time this covenant was written.

James' Future Wife

I pray for James' wife, wherever she is right now. Protect her and I plead the blood of Jesus over her. I call her in at an early age to become a Proverbs woman. I call forth a righteous child. A child who fears the Lord and walks in His ways. May her hands be blessed and may her beauty on the outside be just as great on the inside. I declare this child to be blessed coming in and blessed going out. I call and declare a bride for my son, James.

Now back in these days, I didn't even understand the power of declaring God's word. Declaring and decreeing has become a revelation in the last seven or eight years. However, the declaration just came out in the writing by the Spirit of God.

It took a miracle for God to bring this woman to my son. Actually, it took taking the time to sit down and agree with God's word for the perfect wife. It took being very specific in talking to God about things. If your child comes to you and says, "I need a new dress or a new shirt," you need specifics. God cares about us more than we care about our children and their needs. He would like to have a relationship with you about the details of your life. Just like you want to know the details of your children and what is going on in their lives. I have discovered that God wants the best for us.

When James reached the age of about twenty-four, many things had been accomplished in his life. He had traveled to many places and backpacked across Europe. He was working for Scott & White Hospital and finding favor in his job. Many great opportunities had happened though this company, and he realized he was getting lonely. Not being aware that I had written multiple covenants over his future wife, he came to me one day and said, "Mom, I'm lonely. I think I'm ready to find me a wife. I would like for you to write a covenant for me. I have some things I have written on paper, but I want you to write one also. And I want to read it and compare it to mine. Then I want us to both sign it and come into agreement with it. I want God to bring me a perfect wife."

Now, James had said many times that he would probably never get married because he had too much to do in life. But when the time is right, there is no man who wants to live alone. So on August 31, 2010, I wrote a covenant for James.

THE REQUESTED COVENANT
August 31, 2010

Lord, James has come to me and asked me to write a covenant for his wife. As You know, Father, I take these things very seriously. I dare not ask for anything that does not line up with Your word. In 2009, you spoke to me about James' wife and what she would be like. I choose to line up with Your word that You spoke to me that day. So I declare on this day, for James Thomas Zintgraff, the most beautiful and perfect wife to come forth and be discovered. A woman with a heart after the Father. May she blend her gifts and talents with James and together they will serve the Lord and bring many to know this Kingdom Living. They will have many friends as a couple and they will find themselves teaching other couples how to have a blended relationship as they do. I declare this day that James will know his wife is the one that You chose for him. She will have this same knowing in her heart. James will love her as Christ loves the Church and gave Himself for it. She will be dressed in beauty from the inside as well as the outside, and James will never doubt her love for him. She will increase in her love for the Father daily and the fire of God will roll over into her. She will find great favor with our family and the women of the family will say, "Yes, she fits in well and we love her." All of the family will love her and accept her. James will also find great favor with her family and they will approve of him. Their children will be powerful. She will be a good mother who instructs her children well and brings them up as a Proverbs woman. She will always lack in nothing and her children will be intelligent and dressed in fine clothing. James will honor his wife and she will see that James finds favor with God and man. James will trust in her and he will have no lack of gain. She will do him good and not evil all the days of her life. She will have servants and give to them a good salary. She will be known in the city and sit among the elders of the land. Strength and dignity are her clothing and she smiles at the future. She will open her mouth in wisdom and the teaching of kindness is on her tongue. She will understand finances and use wisdom in how the earnings should be spent. She looks well to the ways of her household and her children will rise up and bless her. She will exceed all other women and she shall be praised in the city gates. James will recognize the wisdom in waiting upon the Lord to bring such a perfect bride to his side, the perfect wife to come forth for my son, James.

I bless James with this covenant, oh Lord.

I decree it so.

Be blessed all the days of your life, my son.

Amen

Now James had his idea of a perfect wife also. He gave more attention to the details of her desired appearance. He desired an Italian woman. It was important that she had dark hair and olive skin. (I think he was trying to reduce the chances of having red-headed children.) She had to be beautiful, and she had to be shorter than him. James desired a wife who was intelligent and someone who would love and raise his children the way God wanted it done. He was specific and we put our two covenants together and signed them as well as dated them. What is very interesting is that it was almost two years to the day that Rachel walked through our church doors. James saw Rachel and knew she looked like the wife he was looking for.

Now they had to get to know each other, and that is another story, but as I said before, timing is everything. Rachel walked through the doors and met James on August 26, 2012. Don't ever think that dates are not important to God. I believe God set these dates in place to make it clearer that this was an act of God.

James and his wife, Rachel

CHAPTER NINE

NEW PATHS OF MINISTRY

During the past thirty-eight years, Tom and I have been a part of several ministries. We have found it valuable to write covenants for the church and the plans and purposes that God wants to accomplish in our lives. Writing covenants became a vital part of watching God's word come to pass in ministry. Each time God had a new location for us, Tom and I would come together and seek Him as to where that new place was and how His perfect timing would fit into the plan.

One day, in 1994, when we lived in Fredericksburg, Texas, another change in our hearts suddenly happened by the Spirit of God. Tom was the assistant pastor for the church there and worked multiple jobs on the side to keep us above water. Tom and I were praying over our ministry and we could see very clearly that God was doing a new work as well as placing a new call in our lives. We both knew that things were about to change. Several prophecies had come forth about our call, but one in particular stood out that confirmed we were to move on.

"The way has been prepared. Tom Zintgraff is being prepared, let the ministry begin NOW." For some time now, Tom and I had a desire to move to Brownwood, Texas and be a part of the work God was doing there. We had been waiting for the way to be prepared and we needed to declare and call in our new plan that God had. So that Sunday afternoon in 1994, Tom and I went out to the edge of the city, to a roadside park, climbed up on top of a yellow picnic table and put our hands out toward Brownwood, and called in our ministry to this new place.

We asked God to give us a vision that day also. We wanted clear direction for what God wanted to do with us in Brownwood. So as we stood on those yellow tables with our hands stretched out to Brownwood, we began to SHOUT our ministry into existence and commanded the ministry to come to us.

"Come forth, Ministry in Brownwood!' we shouted. "Plans and purposes.... Come forth!" This was an act of faith that has been etched in our minds.

Jeremiah 29:11 was the scripture we declared that day. It says, "I know the plans I have for you, declares the Lord. Plans to prosper you and not to harm you, plans to give you a hope and a future."

75

God honored that act of faith and obedience. Within a few weeks, we got a call from Brownwood that a position had opened at Living Word Church. As an act of faith, I had already begun to pack my bags and box up things. Sometimes these little acts just help with your faith as you walk through things. Most people have dreams and visions deep inside, but never take an act of faith to call it in or write it down and line it up with God's word. He cares about us, but He has given us the authority and power to move and act.

This was the start of a whole new part of God's plan. We moved to Brownwood and Tom became associate pastor of Living Word Church and general manager of a Christian radio station there. While in Brownwood, we were able to grow and be used in many ways. We stayed in Brownwood for ten years, serving. But after the season was over, Tom and I knew deep down there was a new plan and it was time to move on to a new place.

We began to seek the Lord about how this would all come to pass. We both had the burning desire to move with the new plan that God had. Plans to prosper us and not to harm us. We had a plan to start a new church.

Both Tom and I knew the importance of writing a covenant and how powerful it would be. James, our son, still lived at home and was in high school, so we knew he had to understand what we were about to do and be on board. We needed His unity in our family. Tom and I didn't want division within our family, and it was vital that James was in agreement also. So on May 22, 2003, Tom, James and I came together and wrote a covenant for a new place to go. And at this time, we didn't even know where that place would be, but we asked the Lord to meet the desires of our hearts and put us in this new place in His perfect timing.

Two years to the day, May 22, 2005, the pastor of the Brownwood Church stood in the pulpit and released us to go to Temple, Texas. It took two years for that covenant to come to pass.

The timing was so interesting here… Two years to the day. This is why I have encouraged people to date and sign the covenants they write. Timing has always been a big deal with God, even in the scriptures. If we are flowing and hearing Him and obeying, we are on God's timetable and it goes well for us. It is so fun to look back and say, "Wow! That event came to pass at the most pivotal moment in time!" And you can see how the date corresponds with important events in your life. It's like a document that is dated in time and it becomes a history-making event.

It is wonderful to see the different seasons in your life that come and go, and you say, "Hmm, I wonder when that happened?" Oh my goodness, a covenant was written for this very event just three months ago!

Or two years ago to the day! It becomes a reminder of how faithful God is to hear our requests and answer them. If we don't write these things down, we forget what God did seventeen years ago or thirty-eight years ago. It places things in writing and becomes history in the making. When it comes to pass, your covenant then becomes your testimony!

So many covenants have been written. We have written many for our church here in Temple, Texas, and watched as God has been so faithful to bring them to pass one by one.

We keep one just inside our closet door and agree with it daily. Sometimes Tom comes in and says, "Brenda, this covenant is outdated. Everything on it has already come to pass! We need to write a new one and set new goals and watch what God will do." If you have a church or you are a pastor, I encourage you to write a covenant that lines up with God's word. It will be exciting to see what God has planned for you. God desires the very best for you, your family and His church.

CHAPTER TEN

HERITAGE

*I*n September of 2002, I remember a man of God named Woody Woodson praying for me at church. He spoke into my life and told me that my greatest investment was my children. He also said I would come out of all the past with great joy. Tom and I both have seen such joy from our investments. Covenants have been life-changing and history-making.

Tom and I were ecstatic to have grandchildren, so I began writing covenants for my grandchildren when they were still in their mothers' wombs. Each one of my grandchildren is our gift and heritage. I had to make sure that God's word was set in motion from early on to carry out the perfect plan of God. It is called investing in your heritage.

Camdyn was our firstborn grandchild, in the year 2001. I decided right then to write covenants for each of my future grandchildren (although none of them had been born yet). I went to a bookstore and bought a stack of journals because I was believing for at least five or six grandchildren in my future. This first journal was dedicated to Camdyn. When she is sixteen years old, I plan to give it to her. It is full of beautiful covenants especially for her that line up with God's word. Some have already come to pass and some have not been seen yet. This is part of my heritage. I write and declare and decree as I agree with God's word and watch Him perform it. I got an early start on my grandchildren. I knew that the alive and active word from Hebrews 4:12 was going to go forth and penetrate their hearts as I set it forth in writing. This was establishing a legacy to be passed on through the generations to come.

Several people have asked me how long it takes for these covenants to come to pass. They have said, "Well, what if it takes eight years... or forty years?" I love watching how quickly God's word comes to pass. Most of the time, my covenants take between two weeks and two years to come to pass. Each covenant is different, depending on the circumstances. The covenant for our son, James, took ten years before he was born. It is very easy for me to not put time limits on God because He has been so faithful. I find myself writing the covenants and setting them on the shelf. But if it did take eight years or forty years, at least I had the faith to write it and be patient for it to come to pass. What if I never wrote a covenant for my son? God's plan would have been prolonged possibly. Many people that hear this teaching about covenant writing are so concerned about the time frame. God's timing is so complete. I have learned that trusting God is the key to rest. I write the covenant (or agreement with his word) and I rest in it. It takes all the fret of "needing to pray harder" out of the equation. I'm no longer trying to perform to get my prayers answered. The rest brings peace when you give it to God and trust him at his word. When the covenant comes to pass, it becomes the word of my testimony.

I sat down this past June and wrote a covenant for two of my granddaughters, Camdyn and Trinity. Both girls were spending the night with me. It was June 1, 2015. I told them what I was doing for them and they both sat down that evening and wrote covenants for themselves. It blessed me to see my future generation sitting in my home and writing covenants. Both of the girls' covenants came to pass by September of 2015. Just three months. God's word was going forth and did not return void. My granddaughters were so happy to see the word of the Lord come to pass in their behalf. It has become very valuable in their lives now, as well. Each one of my grandchildren will someday receive a journal in their name with covenants written about them in their behalf. A cherished treasure, since it was written since their birth.

It is so neat to see God's word coming to pass and destinies being changed. Lining up with the plans and purposes God has for you and your family makes your lifestyle so much more productive and successful. His word not only changes your destiny and history, but you come into a place of writing your history. There is incredible peace when you know you are in the flow of His word and will. I encourage you....

Write a Covenant Today

SAMPLES OF COVENANTS WRITTEN

*B*elow are a few samples of the exact covenants I have written. I want you to see the simplicity of how it was done. God saw the heart of desperation and honored His word. It was my first attempt to put God's word into action.

Christy

2 Timothy 2:24 The servant of the Lord must not strive, but be gentle unto all men, apt to teach and patient.
Psalm 18:35 Thy gentleness hath made Christy great.

Ginger

2 Timothy 1:9 For God hath not given Ginger the spirit of fear, but of power and love and a sound mind.

Philippians 1:4 Make her more bold to speak the word of God without fear.

October 29 1982
TOM AND BRENDA

Oh Lord, God, give us a new love! A love no one shall separate from the love of Christ. I will say with my mouth that we shall walk in love! And we shall have the fruits of the Spirit: Love, peace, joy, longsuffering, gentleness, goodness, faith, meekness, temperance, and we shall live in the Spirit. We shall not be desirous of vain glory, provoking one another, or envying one another. But we shall be full of the love and glory of Christ Jesus.

No weapon formed against us shall proper. And every tongue that shall rise against us in judgment, thou shalt condemn. This is my heritage and our righteousness is of you, saith the Lord, according to Isaiah 54:17.

Cause our enemies to be at peace with us! I seek You, Lord and I have found You. I have called upon You and You have answered me. We will walk in the Spirit! In the precious name of the Lord, Amen

1980
TOM

Cause Tom to abound in everything, in faith, and in utterance and knowledge and in all diligence, in love and abound also in grace. Cause him to prove the sincerity of Your love, according to 2 Corinthians 8:7-8.

In the name of Jesus, Amen

January 20, 1998
New Year's Covenant for Tom & Brenda

This day, we claim covenant with You, oh Lord, that according to Ecclesiastes 5:18-28, Tom and I and all our children and family shall properly obtain the gift of wealth that only You, oh God Almighty, can give. Wealth and possessions which enable us to enjoy them, to accept our lot, and be happy to work. That we may seldom reflect on our past – because God keeps us occupied with a gladness of heart. Make Tom and me wise with our wealth so that we are not fools with our wealth. Our appetite will always be satisfied. May our words not be meaningless but may our words profit everyone who hears them because they are boldly spoken by the moving of Your Spirit. Keep us righteous before You, oh Lord. Not over wise, not wicked, but people who fear You, oh God. Give Tom and me and our children wisdom so that we can be powerful. More powerful than ten rulers in a city.

Show us how not to listen or pay attention to every word that people say, or hear servants cursing us, but test us by our wisdom. Cause us to search out wisdom and understand the stupidity of wickedness and the madness of folly. Cause us to please You, oh Lord. May Tom and I be on one of a thousand that is upright. May our face be brightened because of your wisdom! I praise You, oh Lord, for our covenant word. We stand upon it this day.

In Jesus' name, Amen

June 10, 2000
A covenant for my daughter and her husband.

My Lord, God! May this year, 2000, be very happy and prosperous for Christy and Eric. As Eric enters medical school – cause great wisdom to be on him as well as the knowledge that has already been given him. May Eric know and have Your confidence that he has heard Your voice in the choice of medical schools. May great favor rest on him and great authority ride on his shoulders. May he always be the strength of his family because of Your word that resides in him. Place both

Christy and Eric in a perfect home that only You can get glory for. Fill their home with beautiful coverings for their bed and windows. May Eric be in full confidence that Christy lacks nothing. May Eric find only the good in her as she sets about her work vigorously. May she always be at peace in her job as well as her tasks at home. May she never be concerned for the household. And may Eric be respected at the city gates.

In Jesus' name, Amen

July 10, 2000
A covenant for my daughter and her husband.

My Lord and supplier for every need, I pray for Ginger and Tyler in this new marriage that was supernaturally put together by Your hand. May Tyler always walk in the counsel of the godly and seek Your face. May he have a kind and compassionate, forgiving spirit to others and a burden for the lost. May Your joy be his strength and the favor of God go with him everywhere. May Tyler be the head of his household as Christ is head of the Church. May Tyler love Ginger as Christ loved the Church – making her holy and cleansing her by washing her with Your word daily.

May Ginger always honor and respect Tyler. May she watch over the affairs of her household and may faithful instruction be on her tongue. May she go about her tasks vigorously and never fear the winter snow because her whole household is clothed in scarlet and fine linen. May she get up while it is still dark to provide food for her family as well as her servant girls. May Ginger always be of noble character and lack nothing.

May Tyler and Ginger have full confidence in Christ Jesus all the days of their lives. Pour Your wisdom in both Ginger and Tyler.

In Jesus' name, Amen.

August 14, 2000
A covenant for my son, James.

My precious Lord, I come into agreement with Your word for my son, James. This year, he shall enter junior high school with the boldness of God in Christ Jesus. Cause great favor to ride on James. May this favor be great with God and man and every teacher, as well as all those in authority over him. May his athletic ability exceed all those around him because he is the head and not the tail. May he grow daily in spiritual knowledge as well as physically; and may he always succeed in his plans because he takes good counsel according to Proverbs 15:22. May his words bring joy in his reply and may he always have timely words. May his path always be chosen wisely in decision making. May James always have the strength and heart of King David. I speak the joy of the Lord to be his strength.

In Jesus' name, Amen

(After writing this covenant for the medical mission trip to Mexico, James, only fourteen, acquired the desire to go into the medical field. James fell in love with medicine studies and pursued his dream. He works in cardiology to this day.)

February 2001

MISSION TRIP Lord, cause the mission trip to change James and his destiny to serve You. Put in his heart the desire and compassion to touch the lives of others less fortunate. Impact his life, oh Lord. Pour Your favor and blessing on him. And show him his destiny through this adventure.

In Jesus' name, Amen

September 8 2005
NEW BEGINNINGS FOR TOM AND BRENDA

Heavenly Father, we give You great praise for bringing us to this wonderful and beautiful area of Belton, Temple, Texas. We are overwhelmed at all the blessings You are pouring out. The financial overflow is more than we imagined. You promised to meet our needs and certainly You have provided for us abundantly these first two months. We come to You in request for a praise and worship leader for Harvest Church.

We trust You, Oh Lord, to send that perfect person who has a passion for our praise and worship. May this leader be submissive to those in authority over them. We desire this leader to have a heart for raising up new musicians and worshipers. Take all of Harvest Church to a new level of praise through this hand-picked leader. May he find great favor with God and man. And may he have a tender heart that yields to the moving of Your spirit. You have been faithful, oh Lord. Again I say, we trust You to be our source. Give Tom and me direction in how to grow and continue to overflow in Harvest Church. Bring more people who are hungry and thirsty for You into Harvest, and add unto us daily as strong leaders continue to rise up to help set the stage for a great revival in this area. We need Your wisdom, oh God, as we move on. Don't let us become proud. We only want to boast in the things that You alone have done for us. Thank You, Lord! Amen

January 7, 2008
CHRISTY (my daughter)

My Lord, I lift my beautiful red-head up to You. My firstborn child. My true follower of Christ. Increase in her the gifts that are placed there by You: her great gift of discernment; her love for being a mother and wife, oh Lord. Increase her household. Her love to decorate the Lord's house... Pour wisdom and dreams into her that will fulfill Your kingdom. In Jesus' name, increase her joy that has already been strength to her. Increase our friendship as mother and daughter. Be the common denominator of our friendship.

Create increase in Christy's prophetic gifts. I come against all fear that could hold her back from the plans and purposes You have for her life. Cause Christy to speak the word of the Lord boldly. Be her speech and help her to hear You and declare and decree in 2008 all that You have for her. May her husband, Eric trust her and love her with an increase by the Lord Almighty. And place Christy and Eric in a spacious, beautiful home where You dwell with them all the days of their lives. Increase the favor on Eric as he hears You clearly and

How to Write a Covenant

place him where You want him to be as a doctor. Open the doors wide and put Eric and Christy in unity on the job decisions. Increase their finances. Increase their love for You and their obedience, oh Lord. Most of all – put an increase of the Peace of God on their entire household.

In Jesus' name, Amen.

January 7, 2008
GINGER (my daughter)

Oh Lord, God Almighty, the God of the universe, I lay my daughter, Ginger before you. May this 2008 year be of the greatest increase in You for her. Your increase is so beyond imaginable than I could ever describe. Yet, oh God above, I trust You to increase the gifts and talents of Ginger. Even as an artist, mother, wife and child of You, may Ginger find peace and increase in wisdom as Your love abounds in her. I declare an increase of finances. Show Yourself to Tyler in a greater degree. As he opens his mouth and says, "I want more of You," increase in him.

Open Ginger's eyes to see You, oh Lord. Open her ears to hear You clearly. Use her hands to Your glory. Open her lungs to breathe You in and experience Your presence as she walks and sleeps. Increase her energy

92

– yet keep Your rest on her. Change her heart only when You want it changed. Increase what You have already put in her heart.

I declare and decree that my daughter, Ginger, shall declare and decree as never before. Speak to her heart to open her mouth and declare! Show Tyler the effectiveness of this also. Show him how to pray and decree and declare. Move in their marriage a new degree of love and trust. Be in their every breath. Be the Lord of their mind and heart. Create a river of financial flow. Create a river of talents and gifts to roll out of their being, and overflow it to their children. May all who meet their children recognize the favor and anointing of God upon them. Most of all, may Your supernatural peace and rest reside in their home on a daily basis. As they sleep, give them all dreams and visions according to Your word. And may they always lay their heads down to have sweet sleep.

In Jesus' name, Amen.

December 27, 2008
JAMES (my son)

I declare this day a word from God for my son, James.

Cause James to walk worthy of the Lord. All pleasing, being faithful in every good work, and increasing in the knowledge of God. Strengthen with all might according to His glorious power, unto all patience and long-suffering with joyfulness in James. Replace his loneliness with Your presence, oh Lord. Fill him up and prepare James for his precious and glorious wife that You have saved and set apart for James. Bring her to James and put a knowing in her heart that James is the one for her. Be Lord of both of their lives. Become the first love in James' life again. Prepare his heart for a wife. Make his heart soft and pure. Place, Holy Spirit, in James the desire to be alone with the Father and to know the Father. Take away the loneliness because of Your presence that fills him.

In Jesus' name, Amen

January 23, 2009
JAMES (my son)

I pray for James' wife to continue in her purity of heart. Carrying herself with wisdom and strength. Holding an inward beauty as well as an outward beauty. May she serve the one true God with all her heart and be an outstanding mother to the children that she and James bring forth. Make James an excellent father. Give James and his wife a beautiful unity in the Lord.

During these college years, increase his friendship with You, oh Lord. Cause his trust to increase in You, Holy Spirit. Abide in James as he sleeps, and pour dreams and visions into him as he lays his head to rest at night. Awaken him in the night to speak to him, and I declare and decree that James will hear Your voice and always be obedient to Your instruction. Rich anointing on my son, oh Lord! Richness in You, oh Lord! Be the source of James' day. Cause him to rely on You and trust You all the days of his life. May all these things come to pass in this year of 2009.

In Jesus' name, Amen.

March 21, 2011
A NEW CREATION IN ME!

Oh Lord, my God...How I in awesome wonder consider what You really want from me...Do I not fulfill the desires of Your heart, oh God? Take my life this year. Pour revelation into me of how to reach others. I want what You want, oh God! Holy Spirit, put Your passion in me, so that I can pour out to others wherever I go. Holy Spirit, I call for the awakening angel to come and blast into my inner being and into my soul and fill me with Your Holy Spirit.

I want a NEW Brenda this year.....Full of passion for Jesus. A NEW body created by You, oh God ! A new physical body that is dressed in dignity and purified by You, Holy Spirit. Purify my whole body, oh God....that it might bring You glory. I cannot do this in myself. But I can do all things through You. I need You, Holy Spirit. I need You to help me be the wife and mother that I am called to be. Even now, I am still needed by my children and I need Your wisdom in that.

I call forth a passion for Your fire. Not just a flame or a kindle...but a fire from You, Holy Spirit, that burns crazy big and consumes everything around me. I yield my body to You, oh God... Take it and use it. May my physical vessel be full of You.

I declare and call in Your anointing upon my life as never before. May I complement the husband that You gave me with Your power; that Your kingdom will be glorified.

Increase in me...YOU .... oh Lord! Increase in me!

GRANDCHILDREN

*O*ur children and our grandchildren are our heritage. It blesses me to see the next generation carry on this covenant lifestyle. I have shared some of my most precious covenants written over a period of thirty-something years. Most all of these have come to pass and now there are three generations writing covenants out of the Zintgraff family. I am honored that God has given my heritage the revelation of how powerful His word is and the knowing that His word is ALIVE and ACTIVE. After years of writing covenants for my family and friends, I immediately started journals for each grandchild from day one. I am sharing a few covenants that were written for each grandchild. There are more to come.

December 29, 2001
CAMDYN MERCEDEZ

My little granddaughter, Camdyn Mercedez.

It is almost time for you to go back to North Carolina. I call forth the anointing on you. The Holy Spirit anointing, I call forth a Great Favor with God and man to rest on you all the days of your life. I plead the blood of Jesus over you, Camdyn. And may you prosper in everything you set your hands to, according to Psalm 1:3. Thank You, Lord, for Camdyn. Amen.

August 20, 2004
CAMDYN MERCEDEZ

My precious little Camdyn, you are so smart for your age. I call forth this day the wisdom of God to rest on you. I speak the precious word of the Lord to go forth into your life. I call forth a gentle spirit. You, Camdyn, will speak the word of God boldly without fear. Thy gentleness hath made you great! You, my little Camdyn, will prosper in all that you set your hands to and you will have many gifts and talents as your Mommy has. I call forth legions of angels from heaven to protect you all the days of your life. I ask great wisdom from God for your Mommy and Daddy as they raise you. I love you, beautiful granddaughter.

In Jesus' name. Amen

(I have watched, as God has performed His word in my firstborn grandchild. She is almost fourteen years old and has excelled in everything she sets her hands to. She is an "A" honor roll student and is bold as a lion.)

May 10, 2003
TRINITY LEIGH

Precious little Trinity. You will be coming into this world soon. Today is your day. May grandbaby Trinity come into this world with a peace and a rest on her. May the joy of the Lord be her strength.
In Jesus' name. Amen

August 20, 2004
TRINITY LEIGH

My precious little Trinity, you bring such joy. You are an added spice to the whole family. You shall have a love for worship, and my prayer for you today is for the Holy Spirit to touch your lips as well as your spirit; to guide you every day and direct you. May the words of your mouth and the meditation of your heart always be acceptable in the eyes of the Lord. I bless you, Trinity. You shall prosper in all that you set your hands to. May the gentleness of the Holy Spirit always rest on you. In the name of Jesus Christ. Amen

(In this day and age, I was able to see my second-born grandchild while she was still in the womb. It was amazing to watch and pray over a child at such an early stage. She has a tender spirit and finds great favor with her teachers and friends. Today I see His gentleness in Trinity and she has a heart for worship.)

August 26, 2014
TRINITY LEIGH

I lift my granddaughter, Trinity, up to You, oh Lord. She has the gift of beauty upon her that You gave. May she never be vain or haughty or prideful, but always have a calm, quiet spirit. Thy gentleness shall make her great according to Psalm 18:35

I declare this day for Trinity 'JOY' unspeakable and full of glory. Make her heart sing for ' JOY,' for she is godly. Give her a merry heart according to Psalm 132.9.

May her mourning be turned to "JOY," according to Jeremiah 31:13, and cause Trinity to make sounds of "JOY" with instruments of music. According to 1 Chronicles 15:16, cause Trinity to find her "JOY" in the Lord God of Israel. May she raise her voice with a sound of "JOY"!!!

I declare "JOY JOY JOY" in Trinity. As Trinity has been faithful in few things, put her in charge of many things. Cause her to enter into the "JOY" of her master and Lord and line up with Matthew 25:21.

Make Trinity's "JOY" complete, according to Philippians 2:2. Make her to find "JOY" in the Holy Spirit. (Romans 14:17)

And most of all – May the "JOY" of the Lord to be her strength!

Thank You for Your word, oh Lord. You are always faithful to perform it. I love You, Lord! Amen

May 26, 2004
ETHAN ERIC

Oh Lord, I speak great wisdom into this grandchild. Let Your word grow inside of this baby even as it is only four months in his mother's womb. I call protection forth according to Psalm 91 for my precious grandson. Bless this family. Pour favor on Christy and Eric as they raise their son in Your plan and purpose. Amen

December 31, 2004
ETHAN ERIC

Ethan Eric Allerkamp will walk in the wisdom of God at an early age. Favor will rest on him. Peace shall bestow him and blessings will follow him in Jesus' name. You shall be a mighty man of God! Amen.

(My firstborn grandson, age ten now, brought great joy into his family. Ethan is our serious child. He is brilliant and there is a peace that rests on him. He has a passion for knowledge. It is a rich blessing to watch as God's word manifests in him.)

November 2006
EVAN THOMAS

Oh sweet Evan. We already know that you are a son, to be born in February. Your grandfather already prophesied that you would be a prophet. You shall have a great anointing and you shall have no fear. You shall bring great joy when you come into this world. You will be strong and healthy. I know you are being created right now in your mother's womb, for the plans and purpose that God has. I declare and decree those plans to be fulfilled. I speak His peace over you now. Supernatural peace.

February 28, 2007
EVAN THOMAS

Our new little mighty warrior. You entered this world today! Truly a man of God has stepped into this world today. You are surrounded with supernatural peace. You shall move with grace and dignity upon your shoulders.

Favor, favor, and more favor shall go with you all the days of your life.

In Jesus' name, Amen.

(Evan, eight years old, is completely different from his brother. He came into this world being called the mighty warrior. He carries himself with favor and dignity. God has great plans for him. We all recognize the call of God on little Evan.)

January 4, 2009
ADDISON ROSE

I saw the pictures of you today in your mommy's womb. As I stared at the pictures, I saw the beauty and feminine features God was creating. You shall have the gift of beauty, as your name means 'blushing beauty.' But your beauty will also radiate from within. All will know and recognize that the Lord God Almighty reigns in your life from a young age. A great desire will reside in your heart to serve the Lord all the days of your life. You will be bold to speak the word of God without fear, and the discernment gift will rest on you at an early age. You will call your mother blessed and you will honor your father. The mother's instinct will reside in your heart early on.

In Jesus' name, Amen.

May 13 2009
ADDISON ROSE

Well, today is your Aunt Gi Gi's birthday, but you are the topic of the conversation since you are only a few days old. You are a product of grace. Grandma Maltby is here and says, "She will always be ROSE in my eyes."

There is no jealousy toward you from your brothers. They love you. May peace and joy reign in your life. Wisdom will be on your tongue.

In Jesus' name. Amen.

(Addison, six years old, came to know Jesus at an early age. She has great strength for such a little girl and a desire to serve. There is great boldness on her also. She is a beautiful rose in God's eyes.)

January 27, 2014
EZRA HONOR

This is a good day. A glorious day. You came into this world with such a powerful name! Ezra Honor... Our newest grandson shall walk all his days with a good reputation and an excellent character. High morals will be an absolute in your heart as well as a good name. You will carry authority and watch carefully in the spirit realm as a watchman on the wall. Others will respect you and your call and purpose. Your name will serve you well.

In Jesus' name, Amen.

January 27, 2015
EZRA HONOR

One year old today! What a joy you have brought to this family. I declare and decree, by the word of the Lord, that you shall walk in God's word and see the goodness of the Lord pass before you. There shall be no lack in your lifetime. You shall hear His voice clearly and walk in obedience to the Lord! Happy 1st birthday, Ezra.

(Ezra is only one year old today and my sixth grandchild. He is our fearless child. It shall be wonderful to see God complete in him all that is desired of God. These are good days to live in.)

CHURCH COVENANTS

Tom and I have been a part of church most of our lives. Since I discovered how active and powerful God's word is, we have made it a practice to write covenants over our church, wherever we live. We have saved ourselves a ton of heartache by allowing God to fulfill His word for us. I feel, from experience, that writing covenants that line up with God's word can nip so many problems in the bud. Each church has its own personality and situations, whether it is financial or people problems.

We desire the presence of God's glory to be a major part of the flow in our services. We also desire a core of leadership that could help us to grow with maturity as a base. His word has gone forth and we have seen so much come to pass. There is a trust that comes from putting His word into action. It no longer is your responsibility, but God's. It becomes exciting to watch the hand of God do the work for you. Tom and I are able to rest. The ministry becomes fun.

January 7, 2008
HARVEST CHURCH OF TEMPLE

May Harvest Church arise and shine, and may the glory of the Lord rise upon us. Tom and I can see that darkness covers the earth, but may You, oh Lord, rise upon us as Your glory appears over us. May all the assembly come to Your light here at Harvest Church in Temple, Texas. I declare and decree that we radiate Your joy! As Harvest Church increases in wealth and riches, we will proclaim praise to the Lord! All silver and gold shall honor the Lord God, the Holy One of Israel. May Harvest Church radiate the splendor of God's hand. Build our walls, oh God. Cause great favor to ride on us. May the gates of Harvest Church stand open and all will know that these walls are a house of prayer! Establish the Kingdom of Heaven in this place. Harvest Church will be called great because it represents a house of prayer. We are blessed coming in and blessed going out. May our finances be so great that we can continue to support our missions with even greater increase. We shall feed the hungry and clothe the naked. Temple, Texas shall be called the city of the Lord! May all who enter Harvest Church taste and see that the Lord is good!
In Jesus' name, Amen

March 21, 2011
HARVEST CHURCH

MORE POWER.....MORE Glory

Lord, You said that Harvest Church was ahead of time by a year because of our declaration of calling things in. This past year, we have seen increase in our vision as well as our declarations. Harvest Church has found great favor in our territory. The power is being poured into our church and worship services. Tom is preaching and teaching under the anointing like I have never seen before. It's been a fun year because of the financial increase, as well as You pouring Your goodness before us.

I come before You today, to declare and decree a greater increase of Your power. A greater increase of Your anointing for Tom as well as myself. Greater finances as well as an increase in numbers. Multiply us this year....not that we can brag in ourselves—but that others can come into this glory that You have set in Harvest Church. Continue the peace that has been poured out. People need this supernatural peace, oh God. May they continue to find it here at Harvest Church. We love it, oh God... This calling You gave Tom and me. We love it! Increase in us, Holy Spirit, that others will see Jesus and know that the Holy Spirit is alive!

We cannot lead these people or take this territory without You, Holy Spirit. I declare and decree this day a G R E A T increase in all areas because of Your fire in us, Holy Spirit. And Tom and I shall not be moved or swayed by man. We shall only be moved by the Holy Spirit. We choose to move and flow by the spirit of the living God alone.

I call in Your rest as well as Your glory to Harvest Church.

In Jesus' name, Amen.

June 26, 2014
Harvest Church

AFTER NINE YEARS......A NEW PHASE

Oh Lord,

We are in a new phase... A new season. Harvest Church has gone through many changes in the nine years we have been here. You have been good to us. We have found the richness of Your goodness and I thank You, oh Lord, for such unexpected blessings pouring into our lives continually. Even allowing us to enjoy the pleasure of our children and all our grandchildren right here in this city has been a great blessing.

You have amazingly restored Tom's heart and health as we have been choosing to rest in You at new levels. Now we need You, Father, for this next phase of bringing Your Kingdom to this earth – our territory. Tom and I need Your wisdom. Holy Spirit, we need new strength and courage to step over into this outpouring. We shall not be overwhelmed but overjoyed as we watch Your pleasure happen within our territory. I declare that we never step out of Your rest as You explode the new things that You delight in doing through Harvest Church. Tom and I decree this very day to be the open vessels that You can use to accomplish all that You please. Continue to pour the financial blessings upon us that we can help others and support the Gospel even further.

We shall intentionally set our hearts and faces to the plan and purpose You desire to fulfill through our lives. Do as You please in this place as the glory pours into our land. Tom and I yield our lives and hearts to fulfill all that You have for us.

We rejoice in the leadership that has come into Harvest Church. We are constantly amazed and encouraged that so many of the war-torn, and weary were pastors who needed to be healed. Now we find ourselves with a core of solid families who desire Your plan for the harvest of your Kingdom.

We love You, Father, and have enjoyed this new place and land You brought us to. May we never give up or fail You. We will never leave You or forsake You, Lord. May we always find favor with You, oh God. Show us Your ways. We choose to walk in them.

In Jesus' name, Amen.

March 17, 2013
FORTY-YEAR ANNIVERSARY AND COVENANT

Oh Lord, we ask for Rachel Black's hand in marriage to our son, James Zintgraff. She lines up with all the covenants of the past we have requested in a daughter-in-law. May James follow through with God's plan for his life as well. We declare this day that all of our grandchildren grow strong in the Lord, and our entire family continues to prosper and be blessed. No more miscarriages in our family, but supernatural health for our family in the name of Jesus. We desire a great inheritance for each of our children as well as our grandchildren.

There shall be no lack in our family. May our entire family find great favor with God and man. May our desires line up with Your desires, oh Lord. We declare and decree a great harvest come to Harvest Church of Temple, Texas. May the miraculous come forth in Harvest Church. We also desire the overflow abundance to come forth in Harvest Church as Your word is brought forth with a great anointing.

We call forth the leadership to arise in Harvest Church to step up and take responsibility to take Harvest Church to this new level. Bring forth an outpouring of Your glory quickly. We declare salvation to come into this territory. May people come in with a hunger for the

Holy Spirit and His presence. May Tom and I become the covering and the overseers of Harvest Church as it continues to grow and flourish! Give us Your wisdom, Holy Spirit, in how to bring forth much more revelation to give out and teach people as Your kingdom grows!

We need a new place of worship soon for Harvest Church that is sufficient for what You desire, Oh Lord. And may we find favor with God and man and everything in this land as all this comes to pass.

This covenant we lay before You and call it forth in the name of Jesus Christ. Amen.

I had to share this most recent covenant that Tom and I wrote. This is the now happening as I write.

August 28, 2015
Harvest Church
NOW IS OUR TIME

Lord, the time has come for Harvest Church to find a new facility. We have had a beautiful facility in a mall for seven years. However, we have leased the old facility and have not had ownership.

We desire a new place we can call our own. Your favor has rested on Harvest Church. WE call in that same favor of God to continue as we search for a strategic new place and facility. A beautiful piece of property with plenty of land around it for growth, as You add unto us daily. We desire a clean place where the people can worship and praise You, oh Lord. We declare a visible place in our territory that people can see easily Harvest Church of Temple. This shall be the house of God where the hungry and thirsty souls can come to experience Your presence.

We desire something affordable with office space and nursery rooms. A special place for the youth and children to call their own space. We desire to create a beautiful sanctuary that will glorify Your name. "The name of Jesus."

We desire to please You, Lord, and to have a place where the Holy Spirit can be present at all times. Add unto us daily, Lord. Increase and prosper all that Harvest Church sets its hands to. Increase the anointing in our leadership and our body. Continue to teach us how to serve You gladly and with a merry heart. We know that You can already see this strategic place. Guide us to it, Lord so we might own it and give it to You,

In Jesus' name, Amen.

SCRIPTURES FOR WRITING COVENANTS

*T*here are so many different needs that come along in life. I have used all of these verses for my own covenants. God's word is full of promises for every situation. These are only a few to get started on your own. He honors His word.

SALVATION

Romans 10:9 & 10
This is the word of the Lord, that if you confess with your mouth, "Jesus is Lord," and believe in your heart that God raised him from the dead, you will be saved. For it is with your heart that you believe and are justified, and it is with your mouth that you confess and are saved.

FEAR

Proverbs 29:25

The fear of man brings a snare, but he who trusts in the Lord will be exalted.

2 Timothy 1:7

For God has not given us a spirit of timidity, but of power and love and a sound mind.

Isaiah 41:10

Do not fear, for I am with you; Do not anxiously look about you, for I am your God. I will uphold you with My righteous right hand.

DEPRESSION

Nehemiah 8:10

Do not be grieved for the joy of the Lord is your strength.

Ephesians 5:19

Speaking to one another in psalms and hymns and spiritual songs, singing and making melody with your heart to the Lord.

1 John 1:4

These things we write unto you, that your joy may be made complete.

Jeremiah 31:13

For I will turn their mourning into joy, and will comfort them, and will give them joy for their sorrow.

FAVOR

Psalm 90:17

Let the favor of the Lord be upon us.

Psalm 5:12a

For it is You who blessed the righteous man, O Lord, You surround him with favor as with a shield.

Proverb 8:35

He who finds me finds life and obtains favor from the Lord.

BOLDNESS

Ephesians 3:12
In whom we have boldness and confident access through faith in Him.

Ephesians 6:19
Pray on my behalf, that utterance may be given to me in the opening of my mouth, to make known with boldness the mystery of the gospel.

Proverbs 28:1
The wicked will flee when no one is pursuing them, but the righteous are as bold as a lion.

Acts 4:31
And they were all filled with the Holy Spirit and began to speak the word of God with boldness.

PROMOTION

1 Peter 5:6
Humble yourselves under the mighty hand of God, that he may exalt you at the proper time.

Psalm 1:3
He will be like a tree firmly planted by streams of water, which yields its fruit in its season and its' leaf does not wither; and in whatever he does, he prospers.

SPOUSE

Psalm 20:4
May He grant you your heart's desire and fulfill all your counsel.

HUSBANDS

Ephesians 5:23 & 25
Husband is head of the wife, as Christ also is the Head of the church, He himself being the Savior Of the body.

Husbands, love your wives just as Christ also loved the church and gave Himself up for her.

Psalm 128:3
Your wife shall be like a fruitful vine within your house, your children like olive plants around your table.

Proverbs 5:19
Let her breasts satisfy you at all times.

Genesis 2:24
Therefore shall a man leave his father and his mother, and shall cleave unto his wife: and they shall be one flesh.

1 Timothy 3:4
He must be one who manages his own household well, keeping his children under control with all dignity.

WIVES

Proverbs 31:10 -31

An excellent wife, who can find? For her worth is far above jewels. The heart of her husband safely trusts in her, so that he shall have no lack of gain.. She will do him good and not evil all the days of her life. She works willingly with her hands. She is like the merchants' ships: She brings her food from afar. She rises also while it is yet night, and feeds meat to her household and a portion to her maidens. She considers a field, and buys it: with the fruit of her hands she plants a vineyard. She girds her loins with strength, and her arms are strong. She perceives that her merchandise is good: her candle does not go out at night. She layeth her hands to the spindle, And her hands hold the distaff. She stretches out her hand to the poor; yea, she reaches forth her hands to the needy. She is not afraid of the snow for her household: for all her household are clothed with scarlet. She makes herself coverings of tapestry; her clothing is fine linen and purple. Her husband is known in the gates when he sits among the elders. She makes fine linen, and sells it; she delivers it unto the merchants. Strength and honor are her clothing. She shall rejoice in time to come. She opens her mouth with wisdom and in her tongue is the law of kindness. She looks well to the ways of her household, and does not eat the bread of idleness. Her children rise up and call her Blessed. She excels all virtuousness. She fears the Lord.

CHILDREN

Proverbs 22:6
Train up a child in the way they should go, even when he is old he will not depart from it.

Psalm 128:3
Your wife shall be like a fruitful vine within your house, Your children shall be like olive plants around your table.

Psalm 127:3
Behold, children are a gift of the Lord, the fruit of the womb is a reward.

FINANCES

Genesis 32:12
For You said, "I will surely prosper you and make your descendants as the sand of the sea, which is too great to be numbered.

Joshua 1:8
This book of the law shall not depart from your mouth, but you shall meditate on it day and night, so that you may be careful to do according to all that is written in it; for then you will make your way pros-perous, and then you will have success.

Proverbs 28:20
A faithful man will abound with blessings, but he who makes haste to be rich will not go unpunished.

Psalm 1:3
Be like a tree firmly planted by streams of water, which yields its fruit in due season and its leaf does not wither; and in what-ever he does, he prospers.

My First Covenant

_____

_____

_____

_____

_____

_____

_____

_____

_____

_____

_____

_____

_____

_____

_____

_____

_____

_____

_____

_____

_____

Signature:_____**Date:**_____

NOTES:

_____

_____

_____

_____

_____

_____

_____

_____

_____

_____

_____

_____

_____

_____

_____

_____

_____

_____

_____

_____

_____

_____

_____

CPSIA information can be obtained
at www.ICGtesting.com
Printed in the USA
FSOW02n2248020216
16496FS

9 781498 452533